MW01493250

CHOPIN
FANTAISIE-IMPROMPTU

EDITED BY
MAURICE HINSON

Alfred Music
P.O. Box 10003
Van Nuys, CA 91410-0003
alfred.com

ISBN-10: 1-4706-3184-9
ISBN-13: 978-1-4706-3184-0

2

CONTENTS

Foreword   *Page 3*

Context in which the *Fantaisie-Impromptu* was Composed   *Page 3*

About the Fontana Edition of the *Fantaisie-Impromptu*   *Page 5*

Performing the *Fantaisie-Impromptu*   *Page 6*

Practice Techniques for the *Fantaisie-Impromptu*   *Page 7*

Performance Practice in Chopin's Music   *Page 8*

About this Edition and Series   *Page 10*

For Further Reading   *Page 10*

Fantaisie-Impromptu   *Page 11*

Fantaisie-Impromptu (Fontana Edition)   *Page 22*

FOREWORD

Context
in which
the
*Fantaisie-
Impromptu*
was
Composed

If we just shook and rattled the old chains, nothing would move.
One must add one's own link to the chain. The more original
the link, the greater the step forward.

Frédéric Chopin

The *Fantaisie-Impromptu*, now one of Chopin's most frequently performed and popular compositions, was not published by Chopin himself. This was done by his friend and copyist Julian Fontana, who edited the work as Op. 66 after Chopin's death, along with numerous other unpublished pieces. He thus acted contrary to Chopin's expressed desire never to bring these compositions before the public. Only two of the unpublished works, the mazurkas, Op. 67, No. 2, in G minor and Op. 68, No. 8, in F minor, which Chopin wrote in the year of his death, 1849, might have been published by him if he had lived longer.

The *Fantaisie-Impromptu*, however, was written in 1834, together with the four mazurkas, Op. 17 and the great E-flat major Waltz, Op. 18, compositions that show Chopin at the height of his powers. What might have been the reason for his wanting to keep his *Fantaisie-Impromptu* from being published? There can be no doubt that it possesses great musical value. This is proven not so much by its great popularity, but by the fact that it has been consistently included in the repertoires of the greatest pianists. Niecks, Chopin's foremost early biographer, writes:

> Whatever Fontana says to the contrary in the preface of his collection of Chopin's posthumous works, the composer unequivocally expressed the wish that his manuscripts should not be published. Indeed, no one acquainted with the artistic character of the master, and the nature of the works published by himself, could for a moment imagine that the latter would at any time or in any circumstances have given his consent to the publication of insignificant and imperfect compositions such as most of those presented to the world by his ill-advised friend are. Still, besides the *Fantaisie-Impromptu*, which one would not like to have lost, and one or two mazurkas, which cannot but to be prized. . .[1]

In another article he uses expressions like "artistically unimportant," and "imperfect in every respect, inferior trifles" for the posthumous works and says about the waltzes, Op. 69 and 70 in particular:

> The non-publication of these waltzes by the composer proves to me what an excellent judge he was of his own works – a rare gift in authors.[2]

Yet of the *Fantaisie-Impromptu* he writes:

> The *Fantaisie-Impromptu* is the most valuable of the compositions published by Fontana; indeed, it has become one of the favorites of the pianoforte-playing world . . . According to Fontana, Chopin composed this piece about 1834. Why did he keep it in his portfolio? I suspect he missed in it, more especially in the middle section, that degree of distinction and perfection of detail which alone satisfied his fastidious taste.[3]

And James Huneker:

> The *Fantaisie-Impromptu*. . . is one of the few posthumous works of Chopin worthy of consideration. . . Its involuted first phrases suggest the Bellinian Fioritura so dear to Chopin. . .[4]

---

[1] Frederick Niecks, *Frederick Chopin as a Man and Musician*. London and New York. 1888, Vol. 2, p. 270.

[2] Frederick Niecks, "A Critical Commentary on the Pianoforte Works of Frederick Chopin," *The Monthly Musical Record*, 1879, pp. 179–180.

[3] Frederick Niecks, *Chopin*, vol. 2, p. 261.

[4] James Huneker, *Chopin, the Man and his Music*. New York: 1924, p. 241.

Autograph facsimile of Fantaisie-Impromptu, measures 5–8

There is perhaps another reason why Chopin did not publish the work. There was not one but at least two "Fantaisie-Impromptus," and the genesis of the work is an interesting one. According to Arthur Hedley, a well-known English Chopin scholar, Chopin early in 1834 sent his sister an album published by Schlesinger containing his Op. 15 nocturnes along with a number of salon compositions brought out for the popular taste. One of these was the *Impromptu in E-flat*, Op. 89, by Ignaz Moscheles. The resemblance in melodic shape of Chopin's famous composition in C-sharp minor to this impromptu was sufficient for Hedley to assume that Chopin modeled its construction after the Moscheles work. If one can accept this assumption, it is possible to theorize further that a version of Chopin's piece had been completed at about this time (and that Chopin could have shown his sister a first-rate piece borne out of a trivial one). Hedley believes that this superficial resemblance is the reason Chopin did not publish the work–the plagiarism would have been too obvious. However, the same sort of resemblance exists between the familiar *Nocturne in B-flat* by John Field and the Chopin *Nocturne* in A-flat, Op. 32, No. 2, and this did not prevent Chopin from publishing his equally superior work.

Here is Moscheles:

Another explanation was put forward by Ernest Oster, according to whom Chopin felt that his theme bore too close a resemblance to the finale of Beethoven's Op. 27, No. 2, the "Moonlight" Sonata, and therefore would not publish it.

In 1835 Chopin wrote the *Fantaisie-Impromptu* in the Autograph Album of Baroness d'Este. The Album version, showing precise attention to detail and containing a number of differences from the Fontana version, bears the inscription in French: "Composed for the Baroness d'Este by Frédéric Chopin." This probably indicates a paid commission rather than a dedication, and the Baroness kept it for her exclusive use, which may also account for the fact that this work was never published during Chopin's lifetime. This manuscript is not as complete as it might have been had Chopin definitely intended the work for publication (for example, pedaling is limited to four of its 138 measures), but it is nevertheless a more-than-adequate blueprint for any observant student.

During 1834, Chopin's Opp. 13–16 were published. He visited Aachen for the Music Festival and went on an excursion to Düsseldorf with Felix Mendelssohn. He had great success with his Waltz in E-flat major, Op. 18, and played at Berlioz's concert at the Paris Conservatory in December. In 1835 Chopin had a great triumph with his *Andante Spianato and Polonaise*, Op. 22, and in April he made his last appearance in Paris for several years at a Conservatory concert. He made a visit to Carlsbad in July to meet his parents. During a visit to Dresden in September, he met Maria Wodzińska and fell in love with her. He visited Leipzig where he met Robert Schumann and Clara Wieck. Opp. 20 (Scherzo I) and 24 (Four Mazurkas) were published. Chopin became seriously ill at Heidelberg, and reports of his death circulated.

Julian Fontana's 1855 edition of this piece is allegedly based on a manuscript dated 1834. His good intentions in basing his edition of this and several other unpublished works "on original manuscripts with authorization of [Chopin's] family" is evident in his prefactory pages. Fontana states in his preface that he was prompted to publish his edition at the request of Chopin's family, whose members were not pleased by the appearance in print of unauthorized and inexact versions of some of Chopin's unpublished works. His manuscript sources were exclusively autographs, among them pieces which Chopin eventually intended to publish (Fontana does not say which compositions), were it not for Chopin's habit of sometimes keeping pieces a long time in his portfolio out of "caprice ou nonchalance" (lack of concern). Other works he held back out of perhaps an excess of politeness because they had been written as *souvenirs* for friends. Fontana knew the pieces well, having not only heard Chopin play almost all of them but having played them himself for Chopin. He occasionally had to choose among two or three versions and was sometimes confronted by indecipherable handwriting. At times, he had to rely on his memory. Nevertheless, his authorized edition was indispensable if only to prevent abuses from two directions: those by profiteers, who were menancing a true memory of the composer, and those by friends and admirers, who were trading copies, altering them, and playing them badly. In a footnote he mentions a Paris public recital of 1854 in which unpublished works of Chopin were "atrociously mutilated."

Having expressed his noble intention of presenting the public with the authentic versions of Chopin's unpublished works, Fontana proceeded to fill his pages with expression marks not found in the manuscripts – tempo designations and even metronome marks, dynamic signs and pedal indications – and worse, to alter and regularize Chopin's own arrangements of slurs, which are always original and imaginative and contain the most tangible key to his own gracious and quasi-improvised interpretations. And from the evidence, we may be virtually certain that the same heavy editorial hand was used in the *Fantaisie-Impromptu*, for what he must have had available was the Franchomme manuscript copy, or another like it, i.e., one with very few expression marks. In all, one must judge whether it was better to have these posthumous works, the Mazurkas Opp. 66 and 67, the Waltzes Opp. 69 and 70, the superb and still little-known early Polonaises Op. 71, and various other pieces, printed five and a half years after the composer's death in this less-than-perfect form while the manuscripts were still in the hands of the Chopin family, or whether their publication should have awaited better scholarship, at which time the original sources might have already dispersed. I, for one, am grateful Fontana published his edition, otherwise this work might not have been available to the public for many years after Chopin's death. And many pianists inspite of the above-mentioned inaccuracies, will still prefer the Fontana version over the original Chopin edition for some of the following reasons: the Chopin edition has no arpeggiation indicated before the final chord as has the Fontana version; the Fontana in some ways seems more logical. There are other certain touches, such as the shifting of accents in measures 13–22 and 91–98, indicated in the Fontana version – not in the Chopin version – that are decidedly in Chopin's more finished manner.

Evidence points to a manuscript used by Fontana of which two copies existed, one presumably by Marcellina Czartoryska. This copy is listed in the second edition of *Chopin: An Index of His Works in Chronological Order* by Maurice J. E. Brown (New York: Da Capo Press, 1972, p. 92), but its whereabouts are unknown. Krystyna Kobylańska, in her *Frédéric Chopin. Thematisch-Bibliographisches Werkverzeichnis* (München: G. Henle Verlag, 1979, pp. 159-60), mentions a second copy, this made in Chopin's lifetime (in January 1849) by his cellist friend, Auguste Franchomme. This copy bears the title *Impromptu de Chopin*, which may have been added later; it is in a different hand from the *allegro agitato* between the staves of the first measure. Czartoryska's copy is supposed to have borne the inscription *"Impromptu inédit par Frédéric Chopin."* Franchomme's copy, which includes only a tempo indication, some slurs, and a few dynamic wedges, accents, ornaments but no dynamic letter or pedal markings, no doubt faithfully includes all of Chopin's symbols, and many of Chopin's autographs of works in such a median state of composition, even those that were destined for publication, are untitled.

It appears that Fontana added the prefix "Fantaisie" to Chopin's original title of "Impromptu." The work was first performed by Marcellina Czartoryska in Paris, March 1855.

About the Fontana Edition of the *Fantaisie-Impromptu*

Performing the Fantaisie-Impromptu

Chopin often chose tonalities with many black keys for his works, including this piece, which is written in the keys of C-sharp minor and D-flat major. He attached great technical importance to the raised black keys supporting the long fingers of the hand.

This Impromptu is usually played too fast, as an exercise in velocity rather than as the poetic expression of two contrasted moods – that of an *Allegro agitato* (measures 1–40, 83 to the end) and a broadly lyrical middle section (measures 41–82). When played too quickly, the finely etched contours of the swirling passagework become blurred and ineffective other than as a technical display.

The form of the piece is very simple: Introduction 1–4; **A** = measures 5–40; **B** = 41–82; **A** = 83–118; coda = 119 to the end.

After the introductory *forte* octave, the accompanying figure in the left hand begins *sforzando-subito piano*, but a slight *diminuendo* should be made to the beginning of measure 5. This main theme, which is as fresh-sounding as anything in Chopin, should actually be started *pianissimo* with the *una corda* pedal and with a very delicate tone, so that when it returns in measure 9, where the *una corda* pedal should be released, the *piano* marking will then mean a slight increase in volume. As in nearly all Chopin's passagework of this kind, dynamic shading is essential; for instance, in measure 5 the crescendo is only for that measure, and this same procedure is followed in measures 6 and 7: a crescendo is immediately followed by a *subito pianissimo*.

From measures 13 to 24 the melody in the double-stemmed notes should be brought out richly with the thumb of the right hand.

The *più lento* at measure 41 begins *fortissimo* and *pesante* (heavy), after which there should be a *dimenuendo* and slight *rallentando* into the *sostenuto* at measure 43. In these two introductory measures of the *più lento*, the basic speed of the accompanying figure of the *sostenuto* is established; unfortunately, many pianists take the *sostenuto* section too fast and make insufficient allowance for its broad, flowing character. Chopin's use of the term *con anima* at measure 43 indicates an intensification of emotion, not a faster tempo (he uses the word *anima* in the original Italian sense of "soul"). The tempo for the B section (measures 41–82), then, should be slightly more deliberate. This section is rather long and involves much repetition; thus it is all the more important that variety, color, and nuance be employed here in the many restatements of the main theme. For instance, in playing measure 53, which in the Fontana Edition, but for the turn, is a repetition of measure 45, the tenor doubling of the melody in the left hand might be reinforced, beginning with the upbeat A-flat in measure 52. For further repetitions of the measure, right- and left-hand color might predominate alternately, with *una corda* pedal for the left-hand reinforcement, and without it for normal balance.

With regard to the final A section, I should mention that *Tempo I* should be adhered to, with only a little more verve and *élan* (enthusiasm) than at the outset. In measures 118–119 there should be no ritardando; if anything, one should move with headlong and increasing pace into a *molto agitato* at measure 119. The chords in measures 137–38 should be arpeggiated slowly, such as:

Approximately (lento)

(Ped.)

The word "impromptu" comes from a French adverb meaning unprepared or unpremeditated. As used by Schubert, Chopin, Schumann, Fauré and others, it is generally applied to a composition having something of the character of an improvisation but being clearer in form than the fantasies of earlier composers.

When Chopin was at the piano, he always looked as if he were improvising; that is, he seemed to be constantly seeking, inventing, discovering his thought little by little. This kind of charming hesitation, of surprise and delight, ceases to be possible if the work is presented not as if in a state of successive formation, but as an already perfect, precise and objective whole. I see no other meaning in the title *Impromptu*. I do not think that Chopin improvised his Impromptus and the *Fantaisie-Impromptu*, but it is essential to play them in such a way that they seem to be improvised, that is, with some uncertainty; in any event, without that unbearable assurance that a headlong approach carries with it. It is a promenade of discoveries, and the performer should be cautious about giving the impression of knowing in advance what he is going to say, or that all of it is already written down. I like the musical phrase which gradually shapes beneath the pianist's fingers to seem to be emerging from him, to astonish even him, and to subtly invite us to enter into his delight.

Practice Techniques for the *Fantaisie-Impromptu*

1. Practice each hand separately, the left hand in groups of three:

2. Practice the right hand in groups of four.

3. Count out loud as indicated. Work these up to a very fast tempo, then play them hands together like this:

4. Note that the accents which fall on the third count are played by the thumbs. Do not worry if your groups are uneven, but work to play each group as fast and clearly as possible, with a complete rest and pause afterward, and NO pedal. If you think of those sharp thumb accents all will work out well. Keep counting out loud.

5. Now combine into half-measure groups, and concentrate on the thumb stresses:

6. Then in whole measure groups, repeating the measure as in the piece:

7. The other measures of the piece will fall into shape with this method of practice if you memorize each hand separately and practice in the above patterns.

Performance Practice in Chopin's Music

Much of the secret of playing Chopin in an authentic style is simply to remember that his overall level of dynamics is on the quiet rather than the loud side. As Moscheles remarked, "His *piano* was so ethereal that it needed no powerful *forte* to contrast with it." Certainly there are passages in Chopin that call for power and brilliance, especially in the *polonaises* and *scherzos*, but there can never be anything harsh or brutal in Chopin, and the element of virtuosity must never be emphasized for its own sake. In Chopin's music, there is a sensitivity and even a freedom that cannot easily be taught, but rather must be felt and acquired through intuition. Of the *rubato* in Chopin, Moscheles again has remarked: "The *ad libitum* playing, which in the hands of other interpreters of his music degenerates into a constant uncertainty of rhythms, is with him an element of exquisite originality." But *rubato* style cannot be forced in any way; it must come naturally, for it is a matter of feeling rather than thought. And always avoid aiming at any rigidity of performance; it is best to leave a little leeway for spontaneity and imagination. Chopin himself once remarked that he never played the same piece twice in exactly the same way, and the reviewer of one of his concerts in Edinburgh in 1848 noted with amazement that when the applause necessitated a repetition of one of the numbers on the program, Chopin played it entirely differently the second time.

How can pianists expect to recreate such a sensitive spirit as Chopin's when the customary approach to his music is frequently so insensitive? The excessively dynamic playing of Chopin's music by many present-day pianists kills his spirit. The percussive style of the modern pianistic approach is Chopin's death. When you play Chopin, don't be too rough or excessive. Don't "attack" him!

Let Chopin's elusive spirit sing through you from the instrument. Do not try to tell him how to sing. Chopin's music must be evoked from the instrument, not imposed on it by the player. You must yield to him. You must receive from him. Chopin's phrases must often emerge as though they are the result of improvisation. The mastery of his music should never appear to be self-conscious or forced.

Chopin in 1838, by Gotzenberger

It would be idiotic to say that Chopin's music is not heroic, or is not composed in the grand manner. It is, however, a different kind of grandeur from the dynamic heroics of Schumann, Brahms, or Liszt — more flowing, flexible and richer in substance.

Chopin needs to be practiced deeply in the keys with finger-key contact, at moderate speed and with much conscious relaxation. The contrasting activity-repose, inhale-exhale, masculine-feminine aspects of his phrases must be carefully studied.

Yet his music should never sound studied. Often the pianist must seem to be playing without authority and to be as surprised and delighted as the listener at what he is able to evoke from the instrument.

Recently I suggested to one of my aggressive male students that it might make a good credo for him to repeat daily: "My Chopin will be an evocation rather than a proclamation; a persuasion rather than an imposition."

For the editor's generation, Artur Rubinstein was unquestionably the definitive Chopin interpreter. As the last of the great Romantic pianists – although his versatility contradicted such a narrow categorization – he seemed to our time to have been destined for that eminence by innate qualities of temperament, technique and understanding. But he was not always recognized as a great Chopinist. In an interview that appeared in the *Los Angeles Times* on March 15, 1964, Mr. Rubinstein told of his early tribulations in this regard:

> At first I had to fight to play Chopin. They called my playing too dry. The exaggeration and freedom with which a pianist like Paderewski played Chopin was accepted by the public as a standard and made it difficult for us young pianists. Chopin was a sick man, needed money and had to give lessons to make a living. His pupils, with a few exceptions, were all princes, marchionesses and countesses. None of them had any talent. It was the talentless pupils of Chopin who established what was called the Chopin tradition that lasted for a long time. Paderewski became the exponent of the wrong tradition.

Photograph of Chopin, 1849

That "wrong" tradition can still be heard in some early phonograph recordings and to a greater degree in some of the player piano rolls, recorded early in this century which fairly accurately reproduce at least the major characteristics of the famous pianists of the past. It was a tradition in which the idiosyncrasies of the individual "interpreter" came before the wishes of the composer as set forth in his text. Any and all liberties were allowable – in tempo, rhythm, dynamics, phrasing, rubato; even the composer's notes themselves were frequently altered to suit the taste of the performer. Hearing the remnants of some of those "interpretations," one gets the impression that the more distortion of the text there was, the more the pianist could preen himself as an interpreter. Freedom became license, and nearly any excess was admissible.

No one would dream today of calling Rubinstein's Chopin "dry." Nor would one call it strict in the sense that it never saw beyond the printed page. From all accounts, Chopin enchanted his listeners by his poetry, his imagination and his taste. That was also Rubinstein's formula for Chopin. It adhered to the letter while it illuminated the spirit. It represented for our time – and possibly for a long time, thanks to the fidelity of modern recording – the essence of Chopin.

To do justice to Chopin, you must be a pianist, of course, but equally important you must be a poet. It seems entirely natural that Chopin should have been so immediately loved and appreciated by the greatest poets and writers of his day; and how better can we leave him than in the words of Heine, who drew this portrait of him:

> Poland gave him its sense of gallantry and historical suffering, France gave him an airy charm and grace, and Germany gave him romantic melancholy. Nature, however, gave him a delicate, slender, somewhat frail figure, the most noble of hearts and genius. . .There is nothing comparable to the pleasure he gives us when he sits at the piano and improvises. He is then not a Pole, nor a Frenchman, nor a German; he reveals a far loftier origin; you notice then that he comes from the land of Mozart, Raphael, and Goethe – his true fatherland is the dream world of poetry.

About this Edition and Series

The "Anatomy of a Classic" series is designed to enable the pianist to better understand the masterpiece presented through a comprehensive musical analysis. The performer's understanding of the work is also enhanced by synthesizing many of his/her previous musical disciplines that may have been studied separately through analysis, and by placing the work in its proper historical and musical context. This series allows the intelligent pianist to better realize a more stylistically accurate performance.

The author feels that at some point, it is absolutely necessary for performers to study the compositional process, if they wish to realize a more correct performance.

Among the sources at my disposal for this edition have been the Artur Rubinstein edition of this work based on the autograph from the album of the Baroness d'Este; photographs of the Auguste Franchomme copy of 1849 (Bibliotheque du Conservatoire, Paris, MS. 10491); the

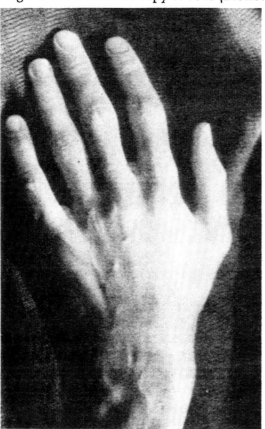

Cast of Chopin's left hand made by Auguste Clesinger

Julian Fontana first edition of 1855; and the Henle edition of 1971.

The Chopin original edition and the Fontana version have been printed together so the pianist may compare both and decide for him/herself which to use. A combination of ideas from both is also possible by having both versions available.

Chopin's pedal indications are identified in footnotes. The other pedal marks in the Chopin edition are the editor's, and Chopin's pedal indications have been incorporated into the editor's pedaling. All fingering is by the editor and indications in parentheses are also editorial. Ornaments are realized in the score or in footnotes.

The editor is grateful to Dr. Thomas Higgins for his assistance relating to the Fontana edition. It is the editor's hope that this performing, analytical, and teaching edition will help the pianist to understand more clearly some of Chopin's creative processes and introduce him/her to this splendid, exciting, and timeless piece.

This edition is dedicated to John Perry, with admiration and appreciation.

Maurice Hinson

For Further Reading

Alfred Cortot. *In Search of Chopin*. London, New York: Peter Nevill, Ltd., 1951.

Arthur Hedley. *Chopin*. London: J. M. Dent, 1963, 1974.

Thomas Higgins. "Chopin Interpretation: A Study of Performance Directions in Selected Autographs and other sources." Dissertation, University of Iowa, 1966.

Edgar Stillman Kelley. *Chopin The Composer*. New York: G. Schirmer, 1913; New York: Cooper Square Publishers, 1969.

FANTAISIE-IMPROMPTU*

Op. posthumous
**BI 87

* Regarding the standard, but unauthentic title *Fantaisie-Impromptu*, see page 5.

ⓐ Chopin left pedal indications at measures 41–45 only: down on first count of measure 41, change at measures 43 & 44, down at measure 44, up on first count of measure 45.

** BI stands for the second edition of *Chopin: An Index of His Works in Chronological Order* by Maurice J.E. Brown. New York: Da Capo Press, 1972.

14

* This measure would have to be [music example] an exact repetition of measure 119.

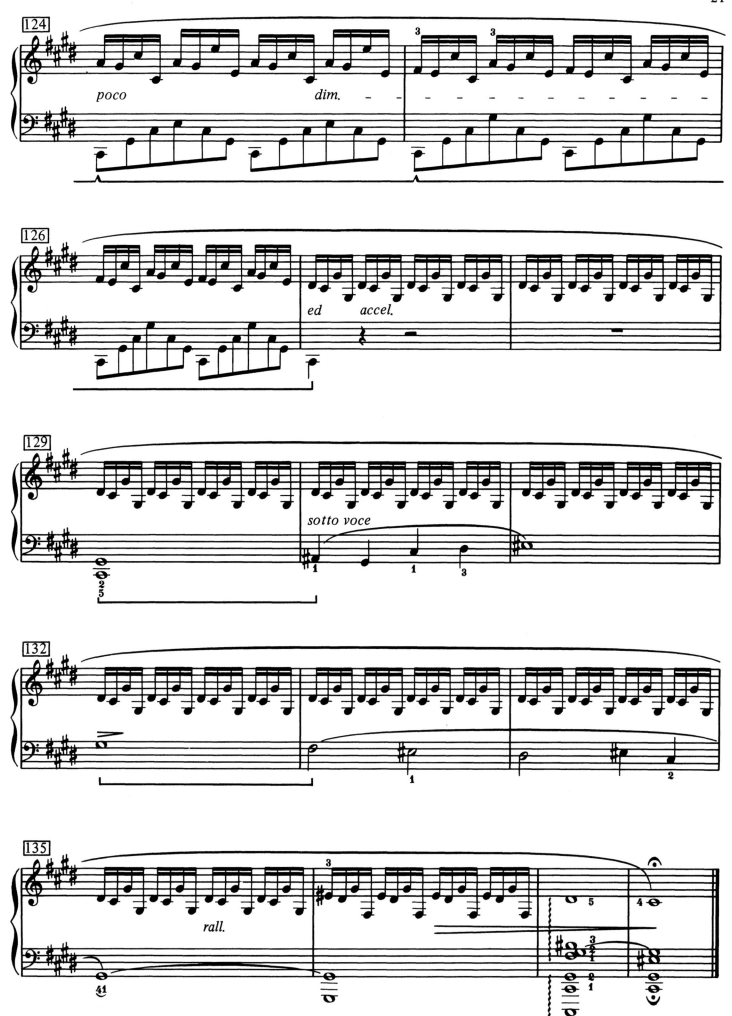

FANTAISIE-IMPROMPTU
(Fontana Edition)

Opus 66 · BI 87

* All pedal indications are by Fontana, as well as metronome marks.

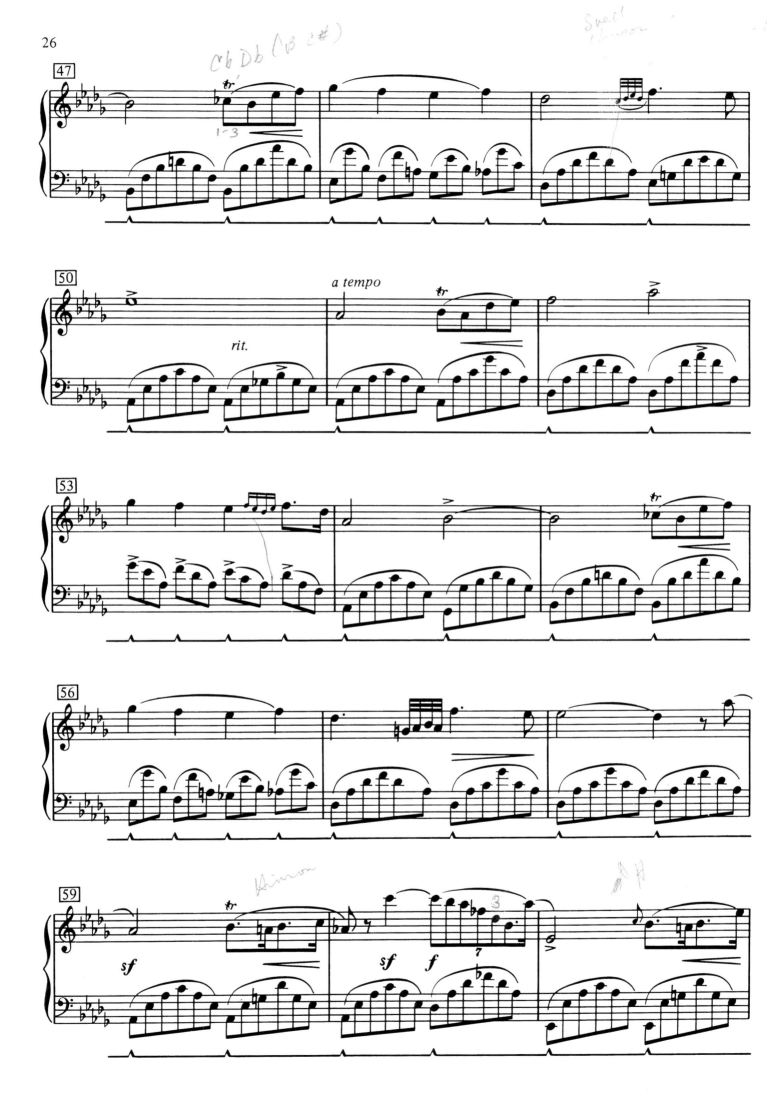

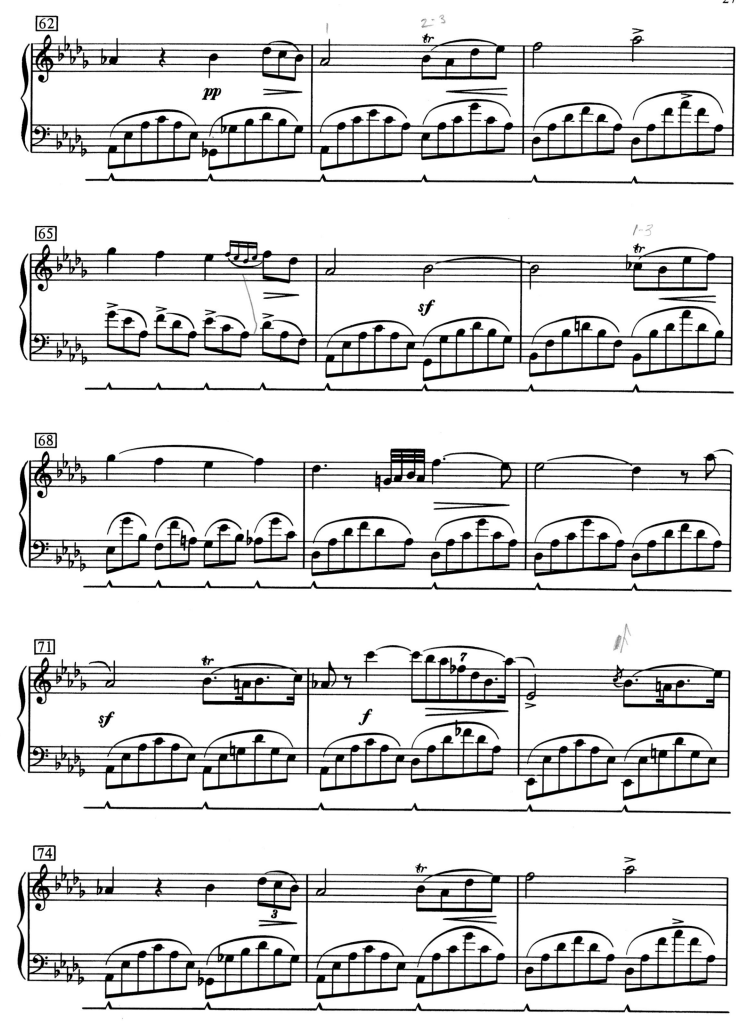

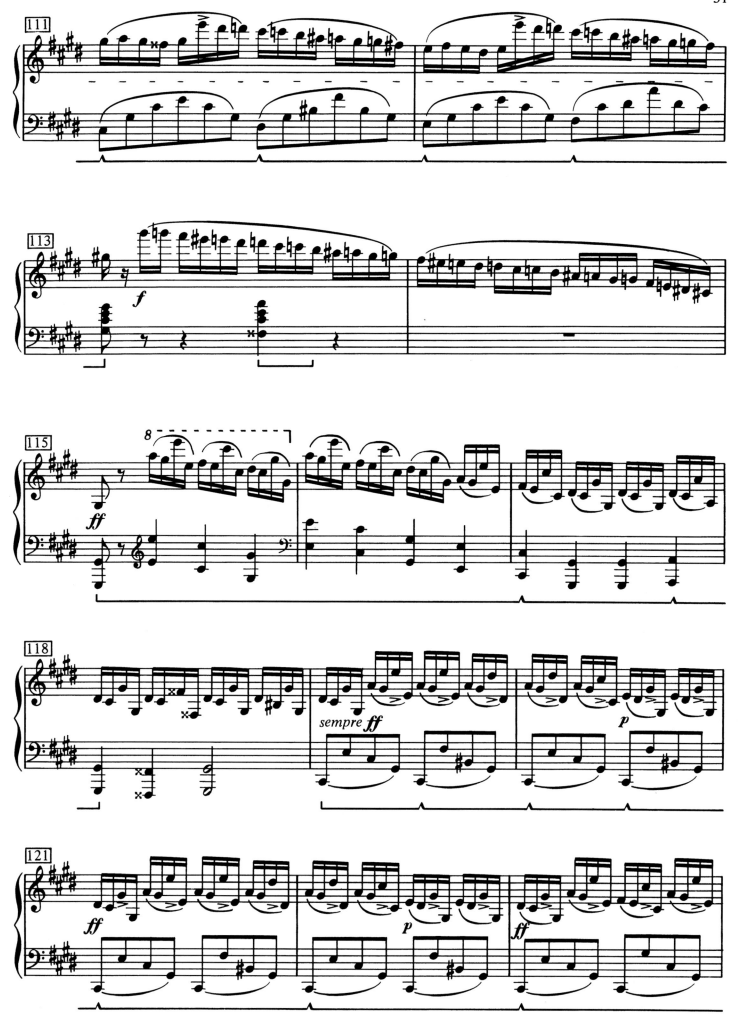

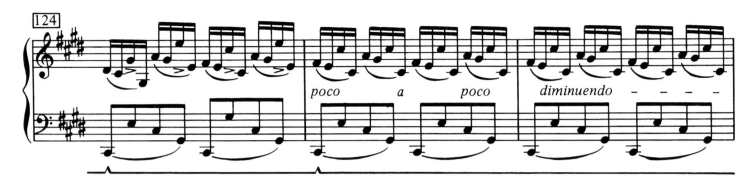